T0130225

"I AM WITH YOU ALWAYS"

A True Story of a Supernatural Encounter with JESUS

PERLA APOLONIO

WESTBOW
PRESS®
A DIVISION OF THOMAS NELSON
& ZONDERVAN

WestBow Press books may be ordered through booksellers or by contacting:

WestBow Press
A Division of Thomas Nelson & Zondervan
1663 Liberty Drive
Bloomington, IN 47403
www.westbowpress.com
1 (866) 928-1240

ISBN: 978-1-9736-6866-4 (sc)
ISBN: 978-1-9736-6867-1 (e)

Library of Congress Control Number: 2019909159

Print information available on the last page.

WestBow Press rev. date: 03/02/2020

To you, God's beloved

*God wants you to know that He loves you
more than you'll ever know
and that He is with you always.*

Contents

Introduction

Have you ever wondered if God is real?

Have you ever asked questions like, "If God is real, who is He? Where could He actually be? How far is heaven? Does God see me? Does He know me? Does He like me? Do I matter to Him?"

You might have heard of things like "God is real," "He loves us," and "The Bible contains God's words." But are these really true? Or is 'having a God' a concept that humanity just created in an attempt to give hope to a hurting world?

You may call me Perla. I am an ordinary woman who lives an ordinary life. I am not perfect, nor anything close to it. I have always believed in and loved God, and I have also seen countless miracles in my life. But I never imagined that in one blessed day, I would have the privilege of seeing the Lord Jesus Christ Himself, in person—an event that would confirm with me that indeed, God is real and that He loves us very much.

Jesus appeared to me on June 8, 2014, one fateful dawn when I was not expecting Him. After that event, I started to receive revelations through visions and dreams, which I would also be sharing in this book with you.

Just to introduce myself, I was born in Manila, Philippines. I'm the eldest of five kids who were raised by loving parents. When I was fourteen years old, my dad suffered from a stroke and was in a comatose state for almost a month. After being prayed for by my mom one day, my dad suddenly woke up from coma—an occurrence that the doctors couldn't explain at that time. That was the first of God's miracles that I have ever seen with my own eyes.

Starting that day, I had the privilege to see countless miracles from God—only I got to see them by going through a journey with

God, faced with storms that only He could tame. Even though my dad woke up from a coma that day, there were still countless times when we had to rush him to the hospital after that event. I remember that we would pray that God would spare my dad's life and that we would have enough money to pay for the hospital bills and other expenses.

Those were tough times, days when we didn't know if there would be food on the table and moments when every single coin mattered. It was a journey of going through a difficult season yet seeing impossible situations turned around. I could no longer count the number of times when dad was revived miraculously. God would also always send us angels in the form of doctors, nurses, and strangers who would hurriedly drive us to the hospital, along with friends and relatives who would help, encourage, and pray with us.

I now look back and thank God for this season, which may have been difficult, but caused our family to become closer to each other. And most of all, it was through this season that I had the opportunity to get to know God as a living, active, and faithful God, who is also our very loving Father. My dad had just gone home to heaven, but I'm so grateful that God gave us the chance to still be able to spend twenty-six more years with him here on earth, counting from the day when I saw that first miracle.

I now live in Sydney, Australia.

I have worked in the fields of accounting and IT for the past twenty years. I am an accountant and an SAP-certified professional. My job then was a little technical and not of a religious nature.

***

In February 2019, I left my role as an SAP billing specialist to study full time at a Bible college in Sydney. Please take note however that I am writing this book, not as a Bible scholar, but as a *witness*—who intends to share with you my supernatural encounter with Jesus and the revelations I have received after this encounter, which I learned afterward to be in line with what's written in the Bible.

***

I love my family, and I have friends whom I consider as family as well.

Basically, I live an ordinary life.

I am an ordinary, imperfect woman who loves God and who has always believed that He is at work in my life even though I don't see Him. I never expected that one fateful day, June 8, 2014, the Lord Jesus Christ would appear to me.

I was caught by surprise when I saw Jesus that day. I wish I could tell you that I was in my holiest self at that time. But the sad thing is that Jesus appeared to me at a moment when I was contemplating sinning against Him. And thinking that what I was about to do was not a huge sin anyway, I still continued to do it even after already seeing Him.

That was the day I realized the meaning of *'God's grace.'*

About fourteen hours after Jesus appeared to me, I suddenly found myself having access to seeing the spiritual realm. I never asked for it, but my spiritual senses were suddenly opened. Having witnessed what happens in the spiritual realm, I then realized the truth about sin, its consequences, and the *depth of God's love for us*—a love so great that is beyond words and even far beyond our sins.

After that night, I started to receive messages from God through supernatural means. At times I heard God's voice audibly, and in my spirit, and at other times, He spoke to me through visions and dreams. You could not imagine how shocked and amazed I was when I started seeing these revelations. I couldn't believe that I was actually witnessing these miracles before my eyes.

There were a few times when I was even surprised by the content of God's message. I would then ask Him, "Really, Lord? Why?" But I noticed that every time God gave a revelation, it would always echo or support a scripture from the Bible. Most of the time after I have just seen a particular vision, a Bible verse would then echo in my mind. So, at times when I asked Him why, I would just go back to the scriptures, and would then find that what He has shown me was actually in the Bible. I have included these Bible verses here so that you can also reflect on them.

Initially, I could not understand why I was seeing these revelations. I only realized the reason, when one day, the Lord asked me to write them down and share them with you.

The conversations I had with God, which I am sharing with you in this book, are not meant to be added to or change any of His words in the Bible. I believe that God spoke to me through these supernatural revelations so that He could explain to me that His words in the Bible are true and are still true to this day, and so that I can testify about it. This book contains my testimony.

You might think that the stories in this book are just products of my imagination. But I want to attest that these are true stories and not fictional.

While showing me visions that explain His thoughts and what's in His heart, there were times when God has also allowed me to feel what He feels. I have always believed that God loves us, but when I learned how much He loves us, I was deeply humbled. I never realized how much I have underestimated God's love toward us, in the past.

This book was written for you. Regardless of whether you already know God or have not yet heard of Him, He wants you to know how much He loves you. I pray that God will speak to you and reveal His great love for you as I share with you my testimony.

PART I

A Story of Grace

The Day Jesus Appeared to Me

It was June 7, 2014. My former boyfriend and I decided to go out that Saturday night, after having been apart for six months. We watched a concert and had enjoyed each other's company so much that we did not notice that it was already a bit late, and he still needed to drive back home. It would be a long drive to get to his place, and I was worried that he might fall asleep while driving, so I offered to sit beside him in his car while he drove back. My plan was just to ensure that he was safe and then take the train back home as soon as one was available in three hours.

When we got to his place, we took the cushions off his couch and placed them on the floor of his living room so that I could sleep there for a few hours while waiting for my train. I tried to sleep, but I just could not. I was not sure why. And then I suddenly felt an overwhelming fear, which I also couldn't explain why.

Just before dawn, I took off the blanket that was covering my face, and then I was surprised to see a man in spirit form sitting to my left. He had dark blond hair that went a little past his shoulders. He was dressed in a white robe, and white light was coming from him. I knew then that what I saw was unusual, and yet I didn't move. Instead I just thought, '*Who can he be?*'

I initially thought he was an angel. But when I looked at his face, that was when I recognized who He was—it was the Lord Jesus Christ.

Then I became more puzzled! I wondered, '*Why is Jesus here?*'

And you know what, even though that was the first time I saw Jesus personally—or at least I am aware of—I experienced a feeling of familiarity. It was as if I have always known Him.

I never expected that I would see Jesus that dawn. Well, I never imagined seeing Jesus during my life here on earth! I think no one would. I was surprised when I saw Him, and at that time, I was just greatly puzzled as to why He was there. I didn't move or say a word, fearing He might disappear. I remained unmoving and was just curious about what He would say or do. There was a moment when I closed my eyes and opened them again to check if it was just my imagination. And He was still there. He stayed there for the next ten minutes.

Without looking at Jesus directly, I asked Him, "Lord, why are You here?"

Shamefully, it was not a question of, *'What would you like me to do for You today, Lord?'* Instead, it was a question of *'Of all the days, Lord, why do You appear to me now, at such a time when I just wanted to briefly hide from You?'*

Then He disappeared.

You see, I missed my ex-boyfriend, and at that time I was feeling tempted to spend just a few intimate moments with him before I take the train back.

***

I understand that expressing affection towards the person we're dating is normal, and how each one does it is already personal to each one. I respect each one's personal space and I am not here to persuade anyone into conducting relationships a certain way.

I come from a cultural background that is a bit traditional, so for the purpose of conforming to it, I have opted to save myself for marriage. It's a personal choice. I'm not here to endorse it or to encourage everyone to do the same. My only intention is to share with you what I went through that fateful day, and what I believe God has taught me through it.

It's not easy for me to share with you what happened that day. If I had a choice, I'd rather not bring it up, however, I felt compelled to because this was the platform God used so that He would be able to explain to me this message—*that He loves us so much*. God loves us so much that He sacrificed Himself and died on the cross so that each one of us will be saved. I hope you can bear with me as I share with you how God has explained this revelation to me.

***

That dawn, I had the greatest privilege of seeing the Lord Jesus Christ in person. I was worried because I didn't think that He would agree with what I was about to do. But regardless, I still proceeded with my plan. I was intimate with my boyfriend, to a certain degree. Not completely. I still tried to have restrictions hoping that I'd still be able to observe abstinence as much as possible. And I thought that I still complied with the personal boundaries I set, in a way. Was it okay? Maybe. In human standards, some people would think that there was nothing wrong with what I did. Or if there was something wrong with it, maybe it's not that big, that God might probably just close His eyes when He sees it.

But you know what, even if it may already be acceptable to some in our society these days, there was still a nudge deep within me that made me feel that what I did was not right. Regardless of the technicalities and what human standards say about it, I still felt that what I did was not pleasing to the Lord.

> Do you not know that your bodies are temples of the Holy Spirit, who is in you, whom you have received from God? You are not your own; you were bought at a price. Therefore honor God with your bodies.
>
> —1 Corinthians 6:19–20 (NIV)

A Taste of Death

It was not the first time I was in that situation. I had repeatedly committed the same offense prior to my encounter with Jesus that dawn. I went to church that Sunday night disheartened because I felt that I had offended God, again.

When I entered the church that night, I noticed that something seemed strange.

Before that day, whenever I entered a church building, I always felt a holy presence in the place. I had never recognized it before though. I only became aware of it that night when I suddenly felt its *absence*. When I entered the church building that night, it suddenly felt like I was only entering an ordinary building, like a mall or an office building. I could no longer feel the holy presence in the place. I was alarmed. I was not sure what had happened. That was when I realized that God's presence has always been with me, but at that time, it was gone.

> But your iniquities have separated you from your God; your sins have hidden His face from you, so that He will not hear.
>
> —Isaiah 59:2 (NIV)

And then, I noticed that the way I see things became different. I could see the physical things, like church walls and the people. But in addition to the physical things, I could also see something else—the spiritual realm. It was like there used to be an invisible ceiling on top of me that restricted my eyes to only see the physical things here on earth, but at that time, that covering was removed. The spiritual realm looked like another dimension that has always been present and coexisting with the physical realm, which I just couldn't see before. And it was even visually clearer than the physical realm. All of a sudden, heaven seemed to be very near—like its floor seemed to only be a few meters above the ground. Also, I suddenly could sense that God was very close to us and that He was gigantic.

Then a small voice inside of me steered my thoughts and made me realize how little I am compared to the planet on which I am standing. I looked up and did not see God visibly, but I could sense that He was looking down on earth, and His expanse was far bigger than the size of the earth, and far beyond what my eyes could reach. It's as if I, a small dot, was standing on earth and was looking up to see that there was a big God who was watching us back.

> Who is like the Lord our God, the One who sits enthroned on high, who stoops down to look on the heavens and the Earth?
>
> —Psalm 113:5–6 (NIV)

And then suddenly, I felt like there used to be a supernatural cord that connected me to God, who is the source of life, but that cord was then cut. Its absence was screaming from inside of me, which made me feel like I was dying. I could see the people around me, and I knew that they were connected to God. But the terrifying thing is that at that time, I felt that I was no longer one of them. I was no longer connected to God.

> Through him all things were made; without him nothing was made that has been made. In him was life, and that life was the light of all mankind.
>
> —John 1:3–4 (NIV)

In that moment, I also got a revelation of God's ruling, in all His majesty, over all the earth—but then seeing it from the vantage point of an outsider. It was very frightening. I realized then that the purpose of my very existence is *to be under God's Lordship*. The terrifying part however was that I only had this realization when I was no longer part of it.

> They will be punished with everlasting destruction and shut out from the presence of the Lord and from the glory of his might.
>
> –2 Thessalonians 1:9 (NIV)

In addition to being cut off from God's presence at that time, I also felt separated from the people around me. I could see them, but it's as if there was a shield that was separating me from them.

At that very moment, I felt alone and separated from God and from everything that surrounded me. It was terrifying. I felt that I no longer mattered. I no longer had value. I felt like a dry leaf that had fallen from the tree and was just waiting to be burnt.

> I am the vine; you are the branches. If you remain in Me and I in you, you will bear much fruit; apart from Me, you can do nothing. If you do not remain in Me, you are like a branch that is thrown away and withers; such branches are picked up, thrown into the fire and burned.
>
> —John 15:5–6 (NIV)

In that experience, I was not even burnt in hell (also described in the Bible as a fiery lake of burning sulfur, a blazing furnace where there will be weeping and gnashing of teeth); I only experienced being separated from God. But I realized that being removed from God's presence alone is already the most frightening thing that can ever happen to anyone. *It is death in itself.* I realized then that suffering in hell is just an additional pain as a result of no longer being in the presence of a good and loving God.

When I was in that state, I also felt separated from all the people around me. This has made me realize that if I was secluded from God and people in this experience, then hell would not then be a place where people can have a party with everyone else who didn't make it to heaven. It's not only a place of no longer being with God and being in eternal suffering. In there, you suffer this pain alone.

That night, I learned the following:

1. that God is real;
2. that God is so big and that He is very near to us;
3. that God is the source of life, and that our lives are coming from Him;
4. that the **state of being separated from God** as mentioned in the Bible, is real; and

5. that being separated from God means being detached from the source of life, which therefore means death.

Because of what I went through that night, I realized that God is the only One we will ever need, and the only One we will never be able to live without.

"I'm Sorry, Lord"

That was the most terrifying night I have ever experienced. I thought that I would already be detached from God forever.

I prayed, cried out and sincerely asked God to forgive me. I earnestly prayed, "Lord, I'm so sorry. Please take me back".

I also pleaded that He would speak to me and that He would explain things to me.

Before that time, I had never heard God's voice audibly, and I didn't know how He would communicate to me. But I just had an expectant heart that I may not know how, yet He would have a way to do it.

So, I waited.

And that was when God spoke to me.

> Call to me and I will answer you, and will tell you great and hidden things that you have not known.
>
> —Jeremiah 33:3 (ESV)

> "When you come looking for Me, you'll find me. Yes, when you get serious about finding Me and want it more than anything else, I'll make sure you won't be disappointed." God's Decree.
>
> —Jeremiah 29:13–14 (MSG)

But from there you will seek the Lord your God, and you will find Him if you seek Him with all your heart and with all your soul.

—Deuteronomy 4:29 (NKJV)

The Enemy Is Real

After that church service, I suddenly heard God speak to me in my mind. You cannot imagine how surprised and amazed I was when I heard His voice.

He said, *"The devil is real, and he wants to destroy you."*

And then suddenly, various scenes in my life since childhood flashed in my mind. In each scene, God pointed out when the devil came and laid his traps, which if I would fall into, were aimed to drag me away from God, which would then eventually lead to my destruction. At that time, it's as if I was given access to a hard drive where I could watch past events in my life, while also seeing where the devil was in each instance. There were heaps of events in my life that I saw. One of these scenes was when I was offered prohibited drugs in high school, which I refused then. When it happened then, I thought that it was just a coincidence that I met someone who offered me something harmful. I didn't know that it was purposely orchestrated by the devil to entice me with it, hoping that I would succumb to his offer. Curious to find out what had happened in other events, I tried to scan my brain as quickly as I could to identify where the devil was in each instance. And then I heard God tell me, *"Hey, don't try to know everything, for you won't be able to contain everything in your brain."* I then realized how little our human brain is, compared to the vastness of the expanse of God's mind. So, I stopped.

> As the heavens are higher than the earth, so are my ways higher than your ways and my thoughts than your thoughts.
>
> —Isaiah 55:9 (NIV)

But I understood then what God was saying to me: that while I am busy living my life, there is an enemy called *'the devil'* who has also been busy executing plans to destroy me.

That particular dawn of June 8, 2014, the devil was there again to tempt me (and my ex-boyfriend, another soul whom the devil hates).

You can't imagine how terrified I was when I learned about this. I thought, *What did I do? Why is the devil after me?*

Prior to this, I knew in theory that 'there is a devil,' but I wasn't aware that he has been actively pursuing me, with an intent to destroy me. I understand that you might find this idea shocking—I also had the same reaction then. However, when I referred to the Bible, I realized that what I saw just validates what's in there. The Bible says that the devil comes to steal, kill and destroy, and that he walks about like a roaring lion, seeking whom he may devour—and it's true.

> The <u>thief comes only to steal, kill and destroy</u>; I came that they may have life, and have it abundantly.
>
> —John 10:10 (ESV)

> Be sober, be vigilant; because your adversary the devil walks about like a roaring lion, seeking whom he may devour.
>
> —1 Peter 5:8 (NKJV)

***

The devil does not only appear in scary forms like what we see in horror movies. Normally, he hides himself in attractive forms so that we would be enticed to take his offers which would lead to our destruction.

And in case you're wondering why the devil hates us so much—*it is because we're God's beloved children.*

Here's a summary of his story:

> *Satan used to be an anointed guardian cherub in heaven. God created him to be full of wisdom and perfect in beauty. But instead of being grateful to his Creator, he became prideful that he wanted to ascend to the highest place and to take the worship that was meant for God. He led a rebellion in heaven in pursuit of taking God's throne. For such, God cast him out, together with the angels who supported him, from heaven and then sent them to earth.*
>
> *Satan and the angels who followed him, now called the devil and his demons, are doomed to be punished in the eternal fire called 'hell' at the end of the world. The devil was filled with fury for his fate, so he has vowed to take with him to hell, the ones loved by God—us. (Ezekiel 28:13–19; Isaiah 14:12–17; Revelation 12) (paraphrased).*

We are all God's beloved children, and because of this, the devil wants to see us all destroyed. He is not only after me, he wants to destroy you as well. His main goal is to get us all to hell. Not because he wants our company there, but because he wants to hurt God by taking God's beloved children into the eternal fire where he's doomed to suffer.

***

But how does the devil take us to hell? Are we supposed to be scared of him? Is God just silently watching while the devil tries to usher us toward this place?

The Penalty of Sin

You might be thinking that the offense which I described earlier may not be that severe, especially in this modern age. Or you may even be questioning if the act which I committed is considered a sin. Or can it just be an acceptable form of expression of affection to someone you're dating who's not yet a spouse? Is God that ruthless that He would punish me with separation from Him for an offense that may not be that grave by human standards? What if I've done worse, would my punishment be more severe than that?

I realized afterward that God made me experience separation from Him that night, not to condemn me for that specific offense, but to make me understand that *sin*, regardless of how light or grave it is, has destructive consequences.

Sin is any act (or even a thought) that does not meet God's holy standard of righteousness. It is any form of disobedience or rebellion from God or desire to be independent of Him. We all do it, in various forms, with varying levels of severity, consciously and unconsciously.

In the past, I believed that heaven and hell exist, but I didn't quite understand who actually goes to heaven or hell. I thought then that we're all sinners, but God is merciful, so He may probably just allow most of us to go to heaven; and maybe only those people who have done grave sins in life (like genocide for example) and did not repent may possibly go to hell.

I knew the concept of 'hell', but I was not aware that we also get separated from God because of our sins. And that night, I learned how terrifying this state is. Being separated from God is like being judged and declared as *worthless* and *condemned*—which is equivalent to someone's end, someone's death. I believe that the word '*death*' (as punishment of sins) in Romans 6:23 refers to this state. Because if you're already separated from God, you're basically dead.

They will be punished with <u>everlasting destruction</u> and <u>shut out from the presence of the Lord</u> and from the glory of his might.

-2 Thessalonians 1:9 (NIV)

For the <u>wages of sin is death</u>, but the gift of God is eternal life in Christ Jesus our Lord.

—Romans 6:23 (NIV)

You may ask if my action that day was really an offense against God. I believe the answer is yes, because it violated God's command to remain pure, in its purest sense prior to marriage. Although I don't think it was God's intent to focus on this specific offense— but to use it as an example, so that He could explain this message:

'that sin, regardless of how light or grave it is, separates us from God.

Since we're all sinners, we're all subject to this punishment of <u>separation from God</u> (or death).

And this terrifying state of death is where our loving God has saved us from.'

***

You may ask, 'How come all sins separate us from God? As it's impossible for us to live a perfectly sinless life, can God not just allow us to enter heaven if we've done more good than bad?'

I want to emphasize that **God is a loving and merciful Father.** He is not an angry God who is always on the lookout for our wrongs and who is ready to hit us with a whip each time we fall. If we dread going to hell and being separated from God, He dreads it more as He doesn't want anyone of us to be separated from Him.

However, it is written that nothing impure can enter heaven (Rev 21:27). This means that we can only enter heaven if we're purely righteous and sinless. This is not because God is unreasonably strict—but because He is by nature, both holy and just.

> Nothing impure will ever enter it, nor will anyone who does what is shameful or deceitful, but only those whose names are written in the Lamb's book of life.
>
> —Revelations 21:27 (NIV)

God being *just* means that it is in His nature to reward good and punish evil. Thus, He will have to punish evil (even the tiniest bit), or else He is not just. (Imagine, if God can just allow sins to go unpunished, then He may just allow Satan to also stay in heaven, whom you and I may mingle with when we get there. Heaven may be chaotic if that happens!)

> Righteousness and justice are the foundation of your throne; love and faithfulness go before you.
>
> —Psalm 89:14 (NIV)

Also, God is *holy*. He is so holy that His angels can't help it but to just proclaim it while they're in His presence. *"Holy, holy, holy is the Lord Almighty; the whole earth is full of his glory,"* declare God's angels in Isaiah 6:3. God is so holy that He cannot be associated with sin. Anything impure which will try to get near Him will be consumed. His holiness is just so perfect that His standard of righteousness is also very high. What may already be pure in human standards may still not be pure enough in the standards of heaven. Again, it's not because God is unreasonably strict, but because God is by nature holy—purely holy. That's why no sin (even the tiniest one) will be able to enter heaven.

God created mankind in His image and in relationship with Him. **We used to be holy too**—until Adam and Eve, the first human beings, disobeyed God by eating the *'fruit of the knowledge of good and evil'* which was forbidden by God to be eaten. That first sin brought poison to mankind which caused us to have the inability to be good all the time. As you know, all of us have sinned. We're still in that fallen state now. No matter how much we try to be perfect, we will never be able to live a completely sinless life. Sin separates us from God—so as sinners, we're all under the curse of death or separation from God. This also disqualified us from entering heaven. And being disqualified to enter heaven also means that we'll be subject to eternal torment in hell.

When Adam sinned, sin entered the world. Adam's sin brought death, so death spread to everyone, for everyone sinned.

—Romans 5:12 (NLT)

> For all have sinned and fall short of the glory of God...
>
> —Romans 3:23 (NIV)

As mentioned earlier, the devil wants all of us to be sent to hell. He brought us all into the state of death when he lured Adam and Eve into disobeying God, and they followed him. The devil still tempts all of us into sinning against God, right now. And then he accuses us before God. Every time someone sins, he goes to God and says "Look, that's an offense against you. So, he's with me, too!" God knows the rules—sin does not belong to Him. As a just God, He would have to execute justice. But as a loving Father, what could He do to save His beloved children?

The only way for us to be saved from the punishment of our sins is if these penalties would be paid for. And since the punishment for our sins is *'death'*, then *'death'* would have to be served.

In the old times, i.e. during the time of Moses, a religious practice was established wherein an animal that's free of defect would be slain and its blood offered, to request for God's forgiveness over people's sins. It was meant to symbolize *death* being served as penalty for sins. Although here, instead of the sinner receiving the death penalty for his own sins, the animal sacrifice takes his place. Without the people knowing, God established this process to paint a picture of something that would take place later on—the day when God would display His great love for mankind.

Two thousand years ago, out of His so much love for us, God took the role of that animal sacrifice. So that we would be released from the penalty of our sins, God Himself paid for it. God, in all His majesty, humbled Himself and became man in the person of Jesus Christ—to shed the blood that was required to be offered and to suffer a horrible death in our place—so that our sins would be forgiven, and so that we won't have to be separated from Him and suffer eternal torment in hell anymore, instead, so that we be allowed to spend eternity with Him in heaven.

***

I never realized how much God has sacrificed for us until the day I witnessed the gravity of the punishment of death that He has saved us from.

> This is how much God loved the world. He gave His Son, his one and only Son. And this is why: so that no one need be destroyed; by believing in him, anyone can have a whole and lasting life. God didn't go to all the trouble of sending his Son merely to point an accusing finger, telling the world how bad it was. He came to help, to put the world right again. Anyone who trusts in him is acquitted; anyone who refuses to trust him has long since been under the death sentence without knowing it. And why? Because of that person's failure to believe in the one-of-a-kind Son of God when introduced to him.
>
> —John 3:16-18 (MSG)

> Therefore, there is now no condemnation for those who are in Christ Jesus, because through Christ Jesus the law of the Spirit who gives life has set you free from the law of sin and death.
>
> —Romans 8:1-2 (NIV)

Since the children have flesh and blood, he too shared in their humanity so that by his death he might break the power of him who holds the power of death—that is, the devil—and free those who all their lives were held in slavery by their fear of death.

—Hebrews 2:14-15 (NIV)

But He was hurt for our wrong-doing. He was crushed for our sins. He was punished so we would have peace. He was beaten so we would be healed.

—Isaiah 53:5 (NLV)

Forgiven

The following day, I was inside my room at home, still thinking about my offense when this thought came to my mind, *'I wonder if God has already forgiven me.'*

Of course, I wasn't expecting any word from God at that time. But I was surprised when right then, I heard an audible voice of a man who said, *"I forgive you."* It was a deep voice of a man in authority, whose tone was not angry. It was the voice of a Father.

I was perplexed. I thought, *Did I just hear God's voice?!?!?!*

I couldn't believe it!

I was still in amazement for hearing God's voice, when I realized that God did not just allow me to hear His audible voice— He has forgiven me of my sins! God has forgiven me! It means that no matter what I've done in the past, it would no longer be a wall between us. And God would no longer remember it nor remind me of it anymore.

I am just in awe of His goodness. *Thank You, Lord! Thank You for Your grace.*

That day, I realized that God is a forgiving God.

So, if there is anything which you've done that you think has separated you from Him—no matter what it is, no matter how grave it is—know that there is no sin that God cannot forgive. Please don't hesitate to go back to Him. He loves you so much, and He's waiting for you.

Repent, then, and turn to God, so that your sins may be wiped out, that times of refreshing may come from the Lord.

—Acts 3:19 (NIV)

But if we confess our sins to Him, He is faithful and just to forgive us our sins and to cleanse us from all wickedness.

—1 John 1:9 (NLT)

All the tax-gatherers and sinners were coming to hear Jesus. The proud religious law-keepers and the teachers of the Law began to speak against Him. They said, "This man receives sinners and eats with them." Then Jesus told them a picture-story, saying, "What if one of you had one hundred sheep and you lost one of them? Would you not leave the ninety-nine in the country and go back and look for the one which was lost until you find it? When you find it, you are happy as you carry it back on your shoulders. Then you would go to your house and call your friends and neighbors. You would say to them, 'Be happy with me because I have found my sheep that was lost.' I tell you, <u>there will be more joy in heaven because of one sinner who is sorry for his sins and turns from them</u>, than for ninety-nine people right with God who do not have sins to be sorry for.

—Luke 15:1–7 (NLV)

So he returned home to his father. And while he was still a long way off, his father saw him coming. Filled with love and compassion, he ran to his son, embraced him, and kissed him. His son said to him, "Father, I have sinned against both heaven and you, and I am no longer worthy of being called your son." But his father said to the servants, "Quick! Bring the finest robe in the house and put it on him. Get a ring for his finger and sandals for his feet. And kill the calf we have been fattening. We must celebrate with a feast, for this son of mine was dead and has now returned to life. He was lost, but now he is found." So the party began.

—Luke 15:20–24 (NLT)

Saved from Hell

A few days later, I started seeing *visions*.

Seeing a vision is like having a dream—you see scenes being flashed before your eyes, but at a state when you are awake.

> And afterward, I will pour out my Spirit on all people. Your sons and daughters will prophesy, your old men will dream dreams, your young men will see visions.
>
> —Joel 2:28 (NIV)

I was in the kitchen washing the dishes when I saw this first vision:

> *I saw a vision of myself in a courtroom. The devil was beside me, and he was laughing and mocking me because of the sin I had committed. His laughter meant that because I had sinned, he had proper claims against me. And there was no way I would be able to deny it. I had sinned—period. It was terrifying. God knows the punishment that was waiting for me.*
>
> *But while I was there waiting for my verdict, Jesus suddenly stepped in. He then said to the devil,* **"Don't touch her. It's on Me."**

My Lord…

I was speechless.

Do you know how it feels to be proven guilty in court but

has been acquitted because someone else vicariously served your penalty? I saw it. And I was the one who was spared.

I have heard at church countless times that our Lord Jesus Christ has saved us from our sins by dying on the cross. I have seen countless times the movies about how He was betrayed, spit on, whipped mercilessly, shamed, crowned with thorns, and crucified when He did not deserve any of it. I have always thought that despite the cost, He still chose to give His life for the salvation of mankind. What I never realized, was the part which I played in putting Him there.

Until that day, I never recognized that He chose to die a painful death on that cross, for me.

As you read John 3:16, I pray that God will reveal to you how much He personally loves you—a love so immeasurably great that has compelled Him to take that cross.

> For God so loved the world, that He gave His one and only Son, that whoever believes in Him shall not perish, but have eternal life.
>
> —John 3:16 (NIV)

Summary

To summarize, here are the things which I learned in this experience:

1. Sin separates us from God.
2. Separation from God meant being condemned.
3. Since we're all sinners, as a default, we are all doomed to be punished with separation from God and eternal torture in hell.
4. God loves us so much that He doesn't want us to be separated from Him and to be tortured in hell for eternity.
5. So, God Himself became man through Jesus, to pay for the penalties of our sins so that we won't have to suffer this death anymore.
6. The devil doesn't want us to know about this antidote. He wants us to continuously sin, to live independently of God, to not repent and to not accept God's forgiveness and salvation so that we'll eventually be destroyed in hell.
7. But God loves us so much and is still very active today in ushering us to Himself.

PART II

The Messages

Revelations

After seeing that first vision, I then started to receive other messages from God through supernatural means. Every time I receive a message from God, you would always find me shocked and amazed. Of course, seeing them was something I did not expect.

What I noticed though was that each of these revelations would always echo a passage in the Bible. This made me realize that the Bible really contains God's words, and that God's words in the Bible are indeed true and still true to this day. Also, another thing which was highlighted to me in these messages was how much God loves us. I've always believed that God loves us, but I never imagined that He would care for us that much.

In the next pages, I would be sharing with you these revelations, along with the related Bible verses, and the lessons which I have learned from them. I pray that God will speak to you and reveal His great love for you while you flip through the next pages.

Remember Who You Are

It was around September 2014—at that time, I was studying an IT course while also working full time. It was exhausting. While in the middle of studying one night, I felt tired and bored. To kill my boredom and hopefully to motivate myself to continue, I decided to open a horoscope article and began to read the part that described the attributes of *Scorpio*, the zodiac sign where my birthday falls. I thought that this article might encourage me with lines like '*Scorpios* are persevering people,' 'They don't easily give up,' or 'They would succeed in any endeavor they put their heads into.'

While reading the horoscope article, I suddenly heard an audible voice say, "*I abhor it.*"

Huh? I was not sure if I heard it right. So, I went back to reading the horoscope again. Then I heard the words again. "*I abhor it.*"

These words surely would not have come from my thoughts because the word *abhor* was not from my vocabulary. I knew then that God was speaking to me. I immediately then looked up the meaning of *abhor* in the dictionary, and the meaning which I got was 'to dislike or detest something very much.'

I was very surprised! With much unbelief, I asked, "*Really, Lord? Why?*" I thought that I only read the article to be entertained. I couldn't think of any reason why it would offend God.

I knew then that God doesn't like us to consult with fortune-tellers, as it is written in Deuteronomy 18:10–12. But I thought, '*I did not read the article so that I would know my future. I only read it to be entertained. So, why would God detest it?*'

> "When you enter the land the Lord your God is giving you, be very careful not to imitate the detestable customs of the nations living there. For example, never sacrifice your son or daughter as a burnt offering. And do not let your people practice <u>fortune-telling</u>, or use sorcery, or interpret omens, or engage in witchcraft, or cast spells, or function as mediums or psychics, or call forth the spirits of the dead. Anyone who does these things is detestable to the Lord. It is because the other nations have done these detestable things that the Lord your God will drive them out ahead of you.
>
> — Deuteronomy 18:9–12 (NLT)

I then realized that I read the article because I needed someone to remind me of what my attributes are. I needed someone who would confirm my identity.

Horoscopes have grouped the world's population into twelve, claiming that each one-twelfth of the world's population have similar traits and characteristics and that I belong to one of those twelve.

When I read *Psalm 139* from the Bible, I realized why God would detest horoscopes. When God created us, He put too much effort to create each one of us. He did not use a mold to just replicate what He has already created previously. Each one is unique. He fashioned each one of us very carefully and planted special gifts in each one, with countless thoughts in His mind on how each one of us will live the best life and how each one of us will play a unique part in blessing the earth.

You made all the delicate, inner parts of my body and knit me together in my mother's womb. Thank you for making me so wonderfully complex! Your workmanship is marvelous—how well I know it. You watched me as I was being formed in utter seclusion, as I was woven together in the dark of the womb. You saw me before I was born. Every day of my life was recorded in your book. Every moment was laid out before a single day had passed. How precious are your thoughts about me, O God. They cannot be numbered! I can't even count them; they outnumber the grains of sand! And when I wake up, you are still with me!

—Psalm 139:13–18 (NLT)

So, when I tried to seek my identity through the horoscope, trusting that I just belong to one-twelfth of the world's population who have the same characteristics, imagine what my Creator must have felt. What could God have felt seeing me rely on someone else to tell me who I am, when He has created me with so much care. He must have said, "You are far more special than that. I know—I created you."

In case you are like me, who sometimes forgets her identity, here's just a reminder of what God says about you *(paraphrased)*:

"You are my child—the child of the Most High God.
I Am your Father.
Know that I love you." (1 John 3:1)
"I have created you according to My own image."
(Genesis 1:2)
"I have formed you in your mother's womb. You
were fearfully and wonderfully made.
I know you inside and out, I know every bone in
your body;

I know exactly how I made you, bit by bit, how I sculpted you from nothing into something.
Like an open book, I watched you grow from conception to birth;
I have already planned all the days of your life before you'd even lived one day.
My thoughts for you are beautiful, thoughts which you won't be able to comprehend nor count as they're countless as the sands in the sea." (Psalm 139:13-18)
"I have engraved you on the palms of My hands." (Isaiah 49:16)
"I know the plans I have for you—plans to prosper you and not to harm you, plans to give you hope and a future." (Jeremiah 29:11)

I pray that you'll remember who you are. You are unique and very special to God. There's nothing or no one like you. You are God's masterpiece and His most precious child.

God Has a Collection
of Your Pictures

One night, I went to bed with a very heavy heart. I was having some problems at work at that time. I felt so discouraged, and my heart was aching when I laid down on my bed. Before I closed my eyes, I just uttered, "Lord, my heart hurts."

I didn't expect that God would answer.

Suddenly I saw visions of a baby and different scenes in the life of that baby growing up.

I was puzzled. I said to myself, "I think I have already seen this baby somewhere". Then the next scenes were pictures of that infant growing up. That was when I recognized her. *It was me!*

Then God spoke to me in my spirit, "***You were that baby.***"

I was surprised, as I have not even seen any of these pictures before.

At that time, I saw images of myself growing up through the eyes of God. And I was surprised by what I saw—*I am beautiful in His eyes.* He was smiling while looking at me. He has been gazing at me lovingly each day, long before I even had the ability to remember. He is a proud Daddy—a parent who is so amazed at every movement and growth of His child and has kept every picture of her in His heart.

I was stunned. I never thought that God, the Creator of the universe, would be so fond of me like that. I knew that God said that He is our good Father, but I never imagined that He is like any parent who adores his kids. I never thought that God gazes at us like He is our biggest fan. And He is!

If you think that God doesn't know you or that you're too

small to be seen by Him—or if you think that you don't matter—it's not true. God sees you. He doesn't only see you—He's your number 1 fan! You're good enough. He is desperate for you! He has a big smile on His face while looking at you.

I pray that God will reveal to you the depth of His overwhelming love for you.

Oh yes, you shaped me first inside, then out; you formed me in my mother's womb.

I thank you, High God—you're breathtaking! Body and soul, I am marvelously made! I worship in adoration—what a creation! You know me inside and out, you know every bone in my body; You know exactly how I was made, bit by bit, how I was sculpted from nothing into something. Like an open book, you watched me grow from conception to birth; all the stages of my life were spread out before you. The days of my life all prepared before I'd even lived one day. Your thoughts—how rare, how beautiful! God, I'll never comprehend them! I couldn't even begin to count them—any more than I could count the sand of the sea.

—Psalm 139:13–18 (MSG)

How great is the love the Father has lavished on us, that we should be called children of God! And that is what we are!

—1 John 3:1 (NIV)

God Is Intently Listening to Your Prayers

And then another night, while I was praying inside my room, I suddenly saw a vision of Jesus beside me. His ear was so close to me (as close as when someone is trying to hear another person who is whispering). His eyes were closed, and He was intently listening to what I was saying.

I almost fell off my chair when I saw this vision. I instantly had to check what I was saying then. I was not sure if at that time I was asking for something vague like, "Lord, please grant us world peace," just for the sake of making a prayer or if I was even aware of what I was talking about.

At that time, I realized, "Jesus is beside me!" I couldn't believe it! He's intently listening to what I was saying. He's interested to hear what I wanted to say. So, I better say what's truly in my heart.

> When you call on me, when you come and pray to me, I'll listen.
>
> —Jeremiah 29:12 (MSG)

> And when you pray, do not keep on babbling like pagans, for they think they will be heard because of their many words. Do not be like them, for your Father knows what you need before you ask Him.
>
> —Matthew 6:7–8 (NIV)

In the past, after saying my prayers, I would normally wonder where they went. Did God hear me? How far could He be? Will my words need to travel a few miles before it will reach His throne? Will He grant my request? Will my prayer request be in the queue? And since there are heaps of people praying, do I need to wait first as God might still be busy answering the ones who have more urgent requests? Will it then be more effective if I'll just course my prayers through the saints?

That night, I learned that while we pray, Jesus is beside us, intently listening to our prayers. He is that close to us whenever we utter a prayer—so close that He wouldn't want to miss a word. We have His full attention. He's like saying, "I'm here, My child. What would you like to tell Daddy?"

So, ask—ask boldly! Pray for sick people to get healed, pray that family members be saved, pray that marriages be restored and don't hesitate to pray for anything even those which already seem impossible with men. There's nothing impossible with God. And He is just beside you and is intently listening to you.

Then Jesus said to the disciples, "Have faith in God. I tell you the truth, you can say to this mountain, 'May you be lifted up and thrown into the sea,' and it will happen. But you must really believe it will happen and have no doubt in your heart. I tell you, you can pray for anything, and if you believe that you've received it, it will be yours.

—Mark 11:22–24 (NLT)

God Wants to Give the Best to His Children

One time, I was desperately asking God for provision. I was looking for a higher-paying job then, and I was frustrated for not being able to get one for quite some time. I cried out to God out of desperation, and then I suddenly saw this vision:

A little girl was crying and was pleading for milk.

When I saw her, I was so moved with compassion that I would do anything just so that she would have her milk, right there and then!

And then I saw another vision:

My earthly father was walking in the street, seeking and asking around for something I needed. With a pleading and desperate voice who would not take "no" for an answer, he said to someone, "Lala needs it." (Lala is the name he called me).

I felt what my earthly dad was feeling at that time. He had that desperate need in him to give me what I needed. He would stop at nothing until he was able to give me what I needed.

I then understood what God was saying to me at that time. I believe He was saying, "If you yourself could not bear seeing the helpless little girl crying because of lack of milk that you would want to give it to her right there and then, how much more would I feel as your Father in heaven for you? If your earthly dad would do everything in his own strength to provide for your needs, how much more would I want to provide for you as your heavenly Father who loves you, sees your need, and can give you anything? It breaks my heart to see you in pain. I will stop at nothing until I can provide for what you need."

I learned that day that God is our good Father who wants to provide for our needs. He will not withhold anything that's good for us. So, if you ask God in prayer and it seems that His answer is taking some time, don't be discouraged. It may still not be the best time yet. He may still be teaching you some things in the process or it may hurt you if you have it right now. God is good, He wants the best for you, and His timing is perfect.

On the other hand, if you received a "no" from Him, it doesn't mean that He doesn't care. It only means that it's something that may hurt you, or there may be a greater good which He's thinking of—which you may not yet understand right now, but you will one day.

(And if ever you're wondering if I got the job which I was asking God for, I did, and I received it when the timing was just perfect!)

Ask and it will be given to you; seek and you will find; knock and the door will be opened to you. For everyone who asks receives; the one who seeks finds; and to the one who knocks, the door will be opened. Which of you, if your son asks for bread, will give him a stone? Or if he asks for a fish, will give him a snake? If you, then, though you are evil, know how to give good gifts to your children, how much more will your Father in heaven give good gifts to those who ask him!

—Matthew 7:7–11 (NIV)

This is the confidence we have in approaching God: that if we ask anything according to His will, He hears us. And if we know that He hears us—whatever we ask—we know that we have what we asked of Him.

—1 John 5:14–15 (NIV)

Don't worry about anything; instead, pray about everything. Tell God what you need, and thank him for all he has done.

—Philippians 4:6 (NLT)

Nothing Is "Lost" for God

It was around July 2017—I was walking then from my house to my office and vice versa. When I got home one night, I noticed that one of the buttons of my winter coat was missing. The coat was fairly new. I only had it for less than a month, so it hurt a bit to see that something was then wrong with it. The design of the buttons was quite unique that most likely they wouldn't be available in the shops. So, in case I would not be able to find the missing one, I might need to change all of them.

It's not the biggest problem someone would have, but it would still be nice to find it. So I prayed, "Lord, I know that You know where it is and that You can point it to me. Please help me find it."

The following morning, I walked back the same path that I trod the night before, looking at every step, hoping I would find it. And no button was found.

It was already dark when I returned home. By that time, I had already forgotten that I was looking for my button, so heading towards home, I walked at the side of the road opposite to my usual path. I then saw a man who was walking in my direction. Since it was already dark and I feared about my safety, I crossed the road and headed back again on my usual path.

I looked at the sky and uttered, "Lord, You're with me, yeah?"

And just around five steps after I said that, I felt a prompting in my spirit to look at a specific spot in the grass beside the pavement where I was walking on. It was dark, so I couldn't see what was in that location. I stopped and stooped down to look at it more closely and pushed the leaves of grass away to check what was hiding underneath. And guess what I found? My missing button—covered by grass in a dark area and found when I had even given up trying to find it.

I knew it was God's way of saying to me, "Yes My child, I'm here beside you, and I've got everything covered."

I learned that day that nothing is ever lost and is not seen by God.

Are you trying to find something which you think has already been lost? May it be a missing button, a lost son, or love in your marriage—no matter what it is, God knows where it is and how to bring it back.

> Can anyone hide from me in a secret place? Am I not everywhere in all the heavens and earth?", says the Lord.
>
> —Jeremiah 23:24 (NLT)

God Never Forgets a Good Deed

One afternoon while I was just walking out of a grocery shop, God suddenly showed me a vision. It was a vision of a homeless person in the street. And then He said to me, *"I have not forgotten."*

I was speechless.

Years ago, I had lived in Manila. And in my former neighborhood, it was common to see homeless people in the streets. I also didn't have much, but I would normally just hand one or a few coins to help out.

This is not to highlight myself about my giving. What I did was not much. I have even forgotten about it.

But when I saw this vision, I was just amazed beyond words.

I neither imagined nor expected that God would keep a record of that event. I was just so touched when I learned that no matter how simple my action was, God has appreciated it and kept it in His heart. I may have forgotten about it, but He did not.

I hope this will also encourage you while you serve the Lord and His children. Know that the good deeds that we do in secret are really seen by God and are not in vain.

So when you give to the needy, do not announce it with trumpets, as the hypocrites do in the synagogues and on the streets, to be honored by others. Truly I tell you, they have received their reward in full. But when you give to the needy, do not let your left hand know what your right hand is doing, so that your giving may be in secret. Then your Father, who sees what is done in secret, will reward you.

—Matthew 6:2–4 (NIV)

Whatever You Do to Others, You Do to Jesus

Another night, while I was walking on a street in Melbourne, I noticed an old man who was lying on the pavement. He didn't have a home. I also was not in my joyous state at that time, but I just stopped by to say hello.

In our chat, I learned that he used to work as an artist. (I saw his work. He's a gifted man.) He said that he loved his wife dearly, but she already passed away. He missed her so much, so he has just been creating artworks dedicated to her. He shared with me that he had been to prison before and was set free afterward. Just after he came out of prison, he was attacked in the street, and a massive hit to his head caused him an injury, which then made it difficult for him to remember things. He also had suffered various physical and emotional pains all these years.

My heart was just pierced. I sobbed and embraced him. I stopped by to say hello, but I never expected that my heart would be opened and bleed for love after speaking to him.

I blessed him with an art book. It was a small gift, but with a prayer that God would turn his situation around. (I knew that He will, or He may already have.) But deep within me, I knew it was actually me who was blessed that day.

And then one morning several months later, I suddenly woke up seeing this vision:

That same event was replayed in my mind. I was talking to a man on a street in Melbourne. But I was surprised to see that the man whom I was speaking to on that pavement that day—was actually the Lord Jesus Christ.

The King will reply, "Truly I tell you, whatever you did for one of the least of these brothers and sisters of mine, you did for me."

—Matthew 25:40 (NIV)

"Love One Another as I Have Loved You"

One day, I was offended by someone. I was upset, and I wished that there was anything that would be able to calm me down. I said to God, "Lord, I'm upset. I know that You see everything. And I think You'll agree with me this time that I have the right to feel this way." Thinking that I was right, I thought that maybe God would just agree with me and would have no way to tell me otherwise.

However, I wondered if there was still an angle that God saw that I didn't. So I paused and asked Him, "Lord, what do you see?" Then suddenly I saw this vision:

> *I saw a vision of Jesus sitting in His office, the manager's office. At that time, His hands were shaking as He held and read the contract that He was about to sign.*
>
> *Then I saw a little version of myself (maybe the size of a cup) standing at the top of His desk and being gazed at by Jesus. That little version of me seemed clueless about what was going on. She was not even aware that Jesus was gazing at her at that time. She was smiling at an empty space, unaware of the fact that she was about to perish. I just realized that was the situation my little self was in when I saw Jesus shaking out of fear while gazing at her.*

While I was watching this scene, the Lord allowed me to feel what He was feeling at that time. Jesus was full of agony while He was gazing at me. He was in so much pain. His heart was about to explode from so much love for me and anguish for that unbearable thought that He might lose me. What I saw surprised me. I never knew that God loved me that much. Imagine the pain of a Father whose daughter was taken from Him as a captive, and to even think that she would perish in the hands of the enemy was just so unbearable— that was what Jesus was feeling at that time in that vision. His heart was screaming "Ahhh! No one will ever hurt My daughter! I will give anything just to get her back."

*Then Jesus asked the other party in the contract, **"How much?"***

I did not see who the other party was in that vision, but I believe it was the devil, whom Jesus was speaking to at that time.

I was not able to read what the contract stated. But I believe it said, "Your blood in exchange for her blood."

And Jesus signed the contract with so much love.

After I saw this vision, I heard Him say to me, **"That's how much I love you. And that's how much I love him too."**

That day, I realized two things:

When Jesus saved us from hell, it wasn't just out of pity. It was out of the love of a Father who would be willing to sacrifice Himself in exchange for His children's safety.

And as He has loved us, it's also what He wants us to do to others.

My command is this: <u>Love each other as I have loved you.</u> Greater love has no one than this: to lay down one's life for one's friends.

—John 15:12–13 (NIV)

So now I am giving you a new commandment: Love each other. <u>Just as I have loved you, you should love each other.</u> Your love for one another will prove to the world that you are my disciples."

—John 13:34–35 (NLT)

Get rid of all bitterness, rage, anger, harsh words, and slander, as well as all types of evil behavior. Instead, be kind to each other, tenderhearted, forgiving one another, just as God through Christ has forgiven you.

—Ephesians 4:31–32 (NLT)

"But to you who are willing to listen, I say, love your enemies! Do good to those who hate you. Bless those who curse you. Pray for those who hurt you. If someone slaps you on one cheek, offer the other cheek also. If someone demands your coat, offer your shirt also. Give to anyone who asks; and when things are taken away from you, don't try to get them back. Do to others as you would like them to do to you.

"If you love only those who love you, why should you get credit for that? Even sinners love those who love them! And if you do good only to those who do good to you, why should you get credit? Even sinners do that much! And if you lend money only to those who can repay you, why should you get credit? Even sinners will lend to other sinners for a full return.

"Love your enemies! Do good to them. Lend to them without expecting to be repaid. Then your reward from heaven will be very great, and you will truly be acting as children of the Most High, for he is kind to those who are unthankful and wicked. You must be compassionate, just as your Father is compassionate.

—Luke 6:27–36 (NLT)

Forgive

Some years ago, I had a friend whom I thought had hurt me. The blame was not only on her. I also had my share on the cause of the grieved friendship. The last time I saw her, that was when we said our "I'm sorrys" to each other.

Then one day, God just suddenly brought her into my mind. Out of the blue, her face just kept on appearing in visions everywhere I looked. I was puzzled. I then asked God, "Lord, why are you reminding me of her? Would you like me to forgive her? I thought I already have. I already said it before, right? I never wished anything bad to happen to her, and I pray that she'll be blessed. I thought that was the definition of '*forgiveness*'?"

I know that God knows the recesses of my heart and that there's nothing I can hide from Him. So I said, "Lord, I've forgiven her. I tried to. Although I know that you know, every time her name is mentioned, the memory of that moment when she did me wrong still comes back into my mind. I don't know what to do to take this away. I just thought that maybe it would be better if our paths would just not cross again? I don't mean anything harm. I'm just scared that if I see her, I will be reminded again of that past pain."

And then He said to me, "*If you'll see each other in heaven, how will you treat each other then? Will you say a brief hello and then walk the other way?*"

I then realized why God doesn't want us to hold any grudge against anyone here on earth. It's because there's no '*unforgiveness*' in heaven. There, everyone has been forgiven and is free.

And then He said, "*You also sinned against her. You also sinned against Me.*"

After that conversation, I asked God to heal me. The healing was gradual. It took me days of surrendering the pain to God. Until one day, I was already able to send her a message that I had forgiven her. And the moment I did that, I also gained freedom— the freedom to be able to think of her without any feeling of pain. That if I ever see her again here on earth or in heaven, I know I have nothing against her.

Was it me who removed that pain? No. I am not able to do that by myself. I just had to decide that I would be willing to do what God wants, i.e. to forgive so that the other person would be free, and so that I would also be free. And then once I have decided to do it, God then did the supernatural part which I could not do, i.e. to heal my wound.

To forgive is normally the hardest thing to do, especially when we or someone we love has been badly hurt by anyone. I am not saying that God doesn't care about our pain nor the injustice done to us. Surely, He is a just God who will avenge us from any harm done against us. But He wants us to forgive, because He cares about us and He doesn't want us to carry that pain in our hearts anymore.

In case you're struggling in this area, I pray that you will be able to surrender your pain to God and ask for His help so that He can heal you. No matter how difficult the task of forgiving is, the Lord will have a way to help you with it.

For if you forgive other people when they sin against you, your heavenly Father will also forgive you. But if you do not forgive others their sins, your Father will not forgive your sins.

—Matthew 6:14–15 (NIV)

Make allowance for each other's faults, and forgive anyone who offends you. Remember, the Lord forgave you, so you must forgive others.

—Colossians 3:13 (NLT)

Do not repay anyone evil for evil. Be careful to do what is right in the eyes of everyone. If it is possible, as far as it depends on you, live at peace with everyone. Do not take revenge, my dear friends, but leave room for God's wrath, for it is written: "It is mine to avenge; I will repay," says the Lord.

—Romans 12:17–19 (NIV)

Jesus Is with Us Always

In July 2014, a month after Jesus appeared to me, I attended a church gathering where a Filipino preacher would be preaching the Word. I know this man has done so much to spread the love of Jesus in the Philippines and mostly to the Filipinos all around the world. While the preacher was walking toward the center of the platform to preach, suddenly I saw Jesus's face appear, occupying the whole wall of the platform. I was surprised! I saw Jesus gazed at him with a big smile of a proud Father. I was amazed at what I saw, and I was inspired to see how Jesus commended His faithful servant.

After that event, there were numerous times when I saw Jesus in services at church. Over several instances, I saw Him on the platform while we were singing worship songs during the service. He would just be standing on the platform together with other church staff in there. Jesus would have a big smile on His face and would seem to be enjoying while we sang worship songs for Him. This has immensely changed me in the way I worship the Lord. When I learned that Jesus was just there at the front, I would definitely not sing just for the sake of singing. My whole being would just want to surrender and run to my Savior. I would dance, lift up my hands, and sing with the best voice I could offer!

There were other times when I saw Jesus inside the church but in the audience area. One instance, I saw Him beside a lady at church who was kneeling and weeping while we sang worship songs. Jesus's hand was on her shoulder. Without her knowing, while she was weeping, Jesus was beside her, assuring her that He was there and that things would be all right.

There were also other instances when I sighted Jesus in places other than church. One time, I saw Him from our office window, and He was taller than the buildings. Another time, I saw Jesus in our midst when I attended a baby shower for a friend. He was with us when I attended a send-off party for another friend. He was in the garden when I was about to enter our new house. Twice, I saw Him sitting in the back seat of my car while I was driving. (You don't know how shocked I was when they happened!) I also saw Him standing next to my friend in our living room one time.

And there were many other instances!

There was even one morning when I woke up seeing a vision of Jesus standing beside me while I slept. I was so surprised when He bent over and kissed me on the cheek. It was like a scene of a daddy saying "good morning" to his little girl.

Initially, I could not understand why I see these visions. But I just realized that the Lord Jesus Christ wants us to know that when He said, "I Am with you always, even to the end of the age," He meant it. And He has kept His promise.

If you are on the verge of divorce, were unjustly hurt, have lost a loved one, or are suffering from an illness that you think is incurable and you are asking "God, where are you?"—remember His promise, "I Am with you always, even to the end of the age."

And be sure of this: I am with you always, even to the end of the age."

—Matthew 28:20 (NLT)

Who Is Jesus?

You might be wondering, '*But is Jesus really God? Or is He just a man whom God also created?*' I understand that up to now, this topic is still a big subject in various debates. For a long time, I myself also struggled to reconcile this thought in my mind.

In early 2018, I attended some class lectures at church about the book of Genesis. One night, the topic that was being discussed was Genesis 3, i.e. the story of Adam and Eve falling into temptation. As you may already know, in this story, Adam and Eve (the first human beings) were tempted by the devil (disguised as a snake) to eat the fruit from the '*tree of the knowledge of good and evil*,' which was forbidden by God to be eaten. God forbade Adam and Eve to eat this fruit for it would cause them to die. But Adam and Eve still disobeyed God, causing them and all mankind to be separated from God and to be under the curse of death.

I was surprised when just after this lecture, I saw this vision:

> *I saw the earth, with a man and a woman who have just been destroyed. And then I saw Jesus who is bigger than the earth. I saw Him cried out and screamed in anguish to release an unfathomable pain that was coming from his core. It was an anguish of a Father whose two beloved children have just been destroyed.*

I was very surprised when I saw that vision.

First, that was when I realized that indeed, Jesus is God Himself! And that He's the same God who was present when Adam and Eve sinned in the garden of Eden. I will no longer attempt to explain further how Jesus, who is called the Son of God in some parts of the Bible, is also God Himself (as also mentioned in other parts of the Bible). God is so big, powerful and complex—and my human brain will not be able to comprehend how one God is also the Father, Son, and the Holy Spirit. But I'm grateful for the vision which I saw as it has helped me understand that indeed, Jesus is not just part of God's creation, but God Himself in flesh.

The second thing which surprised me in that vision is that I have always thought that God might have been angry with Adam and Eve when they disobeyed Him. But instead of seeing an angry God toward His two disobedient creations, what I saw was a devastated Father who deeply mourned the destruction of His beloved children.

> Through him all things were made; without him nothing was made that has been made.
>
> —John 1:3 (NIV)

> For in him all things were created: things in heaven and on earth, visible and invisible, whether thrones or powers or rulers or authorities; all things have been created through him and for him.
>
> —Colossians 1:16 (NIV)

Jesus answered: "Don't you know me, Philip, even after I have been among you such a long time? Anyone who has seen me has seen the Father. How can you say, 'Show us the Father'?

—John 14:9 (NIV)

"Very truly I tell you," Jesus answered, "before Abraham was born, I am!"

—John 8:58 (NIV)

"This is what the LORD says—Israel's King and Redeemer, the LORD Almighty: I am the first and I am the last; apart from me there is no God.

—Isaiah 44:6 (NIV)

"Look, I am coming soon! My reward is with me, and I will give to each person according to what they have done. I am the Alpha and the Omega, the First and the Last, the Beginning and the End.

"Blessed are those who wash their robes, that they may have the right to the tree of life and may go through the gates into the city. Outside are the dogs, those who practice magic arts, the sexually immoral, the murderers, the idolaters and everyone who loves and practices falsehood.

"I, Jesus, have sent my angel to give you this testimony for the churches. I am the Root and the Offspring of David, and the bright Morning Star."

—Revelation 22:12-16 (NIV)

God Doesn't Only Listen to Our Songs for Him; He Also Sings to Us

Around June 2014 as well, I happened to hear a beautiful love song that I felt drawn to. I love music, so it was not the first time I was drawn to a song. At that time, I didn't give it much thought as to why I liked the song. I just thought that maybe it was because of the melody.

The following day, I suddenly saw a vision of that same scene being replayed in my mind, and then I heard God say to me, **"That's my song for you."** I was surprised, as that song was not even a religious one. It was a secular love song that you would normally hear on the radio. And when I looked up the song lyrics, I was shocked, as the song describes the situation I was actually in then. It tells about the relentless love of the one singing for His beloved (who in that song was me). I have always liked this song, but I never thought that God would use it to explain to me what He feels about me. And when I learned about how God feels about me, my heart was just pierced. I never imagined that God would care for me that much.

In the past, whenever 'God's love' was mentioned, I would just think, "Yeah, God loves us" (plainly). I have always believed that God loves us so much that He was willing to sacrifice Himself to save us. But as to how much is 'so much' or what He actually feels about me, I didn't have an idea. And you might be the same—and like me, you might also just not be bothered thinking about it.

After that day, there were various moments when God spoke to me through songs. They were the same songs I have listened to countless times in the past, but this time, I could sense that God was speaking the words. And when He spoke through these songs, I couldn't help but cry. I never thought that God's love for us would be that overwhelmingly intense. And I never imagined that He is just like anyone of us, a person who cares.

Here are just some of the songs that God used while explaining to me what He feels. There are heaps more, but I just couldn't include all of them here due to the volume. As you listen to these words, I pray that you'll feel in your heart His yearning to let you know how much He loves you.

> *<u>I can't help smiling when I look at you,</u>*
> *To keep from going crazy is all I can do.*
> *I'm so defenseless with you so close,*
> *The walls have crumbled from my body and soul.*
> *To you my life is an open door.*
> *<u>Everything I have is yours.</u>*
> *I'll try to give you everything you need,*
> *But as far as love goes, there's a lifetime guarantee.*
> *<u>Write your name across my heart.</u>*
> *<u>I want the world to know that I am yours forever.</u>*
> *And I will wear it like a shining star.*
> *Write your name across my heart.*
> **"Write Your Name (Across My Heart)" by Kenny Rogers**

> *Have I told you lately that I love you?*
> *Have I told you there's no one above you?*
> *Fill my heart with gladness, take away my sadness*
> *And ease my troubles, that's what you do*
> **"Have I Told You Lately" by Van Morrison**

> *What will it take till you believe in me*
> *The way that I believe in you?*
> *I said I love you and that's forever*

And this I promise from the heart
I could not love you any better
I love you just the way you are
"Just the Way You Are" by Billy Joel

And in case you don't know it, this is a love song
And it comes from the heart of someone who loves you so
I don't always show it so this is a love song
You are loved I just wanted you to know
"This Is a Love Song" by Bill Anderson

And my love, I can't help but smile with wonder.
When you tell me all I've done for you
'Cause I've known all along.
That I owe you the sunlight in the morning
And the nights of honest loving that time can't take away.
And I owe you more than life now, more than ever
I know that it's the sweetest debt I'll ever have to pay
"I O U" by Lee Greenwood

Time, nothing but time to make up your mind
I'll give you all that you need
I want you to know, I'll never let go
Till you come back to me
And even though you're far away,
I am right beside you day by day
Don't you know my love is here? Don't you know my love is real?
You should know by now, this much is true
My love is here for you
"My Love Is Here" by Jim Brickman

Tomorrow morning if you wake up,
And the sun does not appear
I, I will be here

If in the dark we lose sight of love,
Hold my hand, and have no fear
Cause I, I will be here
I will be here when you feel like being quiet
When you need to speak your mind, I will listen
And I will be here when the laughter turns to cryin'
Through the winning, losing and tryin'
We'll be together 'cause I will be here
"I Will Be Here" by Steven Curtis Chapman

No more talk of darkness, forget these wide-eyed fears.
I'm here, nothing can harm you—
my words will warm and calm you.
Let me be your freedom, let daylight dry your tears.
I'm here, with you, beside you, to guard you and to guide you
"All I Ask of You" from *Phantom of the Opera*

I have always thought that these songs were heartfelt, that if they'd be dedicated to me, maybe it would come from someone who may have romantic feelings toward me. I didn't have any idea that all this time, someone has already been loving me so sincerely and has been singing these heartfelt songs for me, the Person who loves me the most, my Creator.

When I felt God's love through these songs, it was so intense that I felt His very being screaming out my name. It's a sincere and undeniable love that was crying out from His core. One of the songs which He dropped in my heart one time was "Truly," sung by Lionel Richie. And as the chorus was being sung, I felt God's heart screaming with the words, "I'm TRUUULLY head over heels with your love!"

It's hard to imagine, hey? The Highest King, the God of the Universe would stoop down and be head over heels in love with us. I know it's hard to imagine; it had also surprised me, big time! I myself never expected that God would love us so intensely that it is screaming from His heart. But it's true. (Learning this made me understand more why Jesus would die on the cross for us—again, not just out of pity, but because of the love He has for us that's screaming from His heart.)

In one of the conversations I had with God, I also learned that His love for us is indeed unconditional. One night before I slept, I said to Him, "Lord, thank You for loving me. But I feel so unworthy. I always fail You. I'm sorry." And then the next morning when I woke up, I suddenly heard the song "*Walang Kapalit*" playing in my mind. ("*Walang Kapalit*" is a Tagalog song that is translated as "Nothing in Return.") I then realized that it was God's response to what I said the night before. The song basically says, "Know that I am not waiting for you to return the love that I have given. I just want to love you, and that's it."

I love singing to God. And in the past, I thought that maybe He would be sitting on His throne listening to me while I sing for Him. It never occurred to me that our King, our God, would be hopelessly in love with us that He also serenades us even without us knowing.

In the past, I also used to think that God seemed quiet, so maybe He was very reserved. But now I realized that God's love for us is undeterred, a love that wouldn't let go—a love that would be willing to fight for and sacrifice for His beloved, like a knight in shining armor for his princess, or a husband for his wife. When God knew that we would perish, He devised a plan to rescue us, and then He sacrificed Himself for us. And even up to now, He is still relentlessly pursuing us.

Every day He says, "I love you."

Every day He sends something that will make us smile.

Every day He sings songs to our hearts, hoping that we'll know that He cares.

For the Lord your God is living among you. He is a mighty savior. He will take delight in you with gladness. With his love, he will calm all your fears. He will rejoice over you with joyful songs.

—Zephaniah 3:17 (NLT)

And I am convinced that nothing can ever separate us from God's love. Neither death nor life, neither angels nor demons, neither our fears for today nor our worries about tomorrow—not even the powers of hell can separate us from God's love. No power in the sky above or in the earth below—indeed, nothing in all creation will ever be able to separate us from the love of God that is revealed in Christ Jesus our Lord.

—Romans 8:38–39 (NLT)

Be strong and courageous. Do not be afraid or terrified because of them, for the Lord your God goes with you; he will never leave you nor forsake you."

—Deuteronomy 31:6 (NIV)

"I have loved you with an everlasting love; I have drawn you with unfailing kindness."

—Jeremiah 31:3 (NIV)

Heaven Is Real, and It Is Waiting for You

It was around May 2015—I was working as a part-time IT instructor at that time. One Saturday morning while I was giving tutorials to one of the students, I suddenly saw a vision of a beautiful, peaceful place that has a ground to step on, has trees around the area but with clouds everywhere. I was amazed. I was inside the classroom at that time, so I could still see the physical things like chairs, whiteboard, and my student. But at the same time, I could also see this place in that vision. It's as if I were in two places at the same time. I could even see some white clouds surrounding me while I was teaching. This vision lasted for almost ten minutes. It was bizarre, but I believe it was a glimpse of heaven.

On another occasion, I was at home standing just around one meter outside my bedroom door when I suddenly saw a stairway inside my room. The stairway had white steps covered with clouds, which ascended from the floor up to the ceiling. And a bright white light was shining from the top of the stairs. I was surprised, as the stairway looked so real and tangible. I thought, *'How come a stairway suddenly appeared inside my bedroom?'* This scene also lasted for almost ten minutes. After witnessing it, I checked the Bible and there was a mention of 'stairway to heaven' which Jacob saw, in the book of Genesis. Could it possibly be the same stairway that Jacob saw?

> As he slept, he dreamed of a stairway that reached from the earth up to heaven. And he saw the angels of God going up and down the stairway. At the top of the stairway stood the Lord, and he said, "I am the Lord, the God of your grandfather Abraham, and the God of your father, Isaac.
>
> —Genesis 28:12–13 (NLT)

And then another night, before I slept, I prayed and asked God if there was still anything that He would like me to add to what I have written in this book so far. I then had a dream that I was in heaven. It was a very vivid dream. It felt so real. And here's what I saw in my dream.

I was in a hallway of a structure that looked like a palace. I saw white pillars and a high ceiling, and the walls and floors were also painted white.

The moment I saw myself in that place, I immediately told myself, "I'm back home." There was a familiar feeling that it's where I have always lived, that I was just temporarily assigned to earth, but heaven is actually my home base.

When I was there, I noticed that there was no more evil. In there, I was able to freely think and talk without any negative thoughts cutting in in my mind. And there, I exactly knew who I am—I am a child of God.

Across the hallway was a garden, and I noticed some people out there, although I didn't have the chance to speak to them at that time.

And then in that hallway, I met a man who looked like a character from the Bible. He had short hair and a beard, and he was also wearing a long white robe. I was not able to ask for his name. Maybe he was Peter?

In the next scene, I saw myself with that same man, in an area in heaven where there was a window. I looked through the window and saw Earth. While pointing to me where Earth was, the man said to me, "Look outside. There's Earth. It is below heaven, and sadly, it is currently full of chaos."

Looking at Earth from where I was then, I saw it as a planet that was covered with dark clouds. I knew then that the dark clouds I saw represented sin, hatred, and suffering.

And then he said, "There's no more of that chaos here in heaven. Heaven is a peaceful place."

Then I woke up. That was when I realized that heaven really exists. And that it is our true home. Our lives here are temporary, but we were created to be with God in His mansion. I pray that we'll see each other there one day.

But there's far more to life for us. <u>We're citizens of high heaven</u>! We're waiting the arrival of the Savior, the Master, Jesus Christ, who will transform our earthy bodies into glorious bodies like his own. He'll make us beautiful and whole with the same powerful skill by which he is putting everything as it should be, under and around him.

—Philippians 3:20–21 (MSG)

There are many rooms in My Father's house. If it were not so, I would have told you. I am going away to make a place for you. After I go and make a place for you, I will come back and take you with Me. Then you may be where I am. You know where I am going and you know how to get there."

Thomas said to Jesus, "Lord, we do not know where You are going. How can we know the way to get there?" Jesus said, "I am the Way and the Truth and the Life. No one can go to the Father except by Me. If you had known Me, you would know My Father also. From now on you know Him and have seen Him."

—John 14:2–7 (NLV)

Jesus Died to Open Heaven for Us

In July 2016, I attended a church conference at Qudos Arena in Sydney. While we were singing worship songs for God then, I suddenly saw this vision:

I saw a vision of Jesus, wearing a crown of thorns, was naked and was full of lashes all over his body. His whole body was drenched in blood, and He was terribly in pain while He crawled at the center of the arena.

Then in the next scene—I saw myself and others behind Jesus, following Him as He struggled to take His steps. It was dark. Finally, Jesus reached His last step. He then opened His arms wide and gave all of His remaining strength to tear the veil in front of us. And then a bright light entered through the tore of the veil—the gates of heaven were opened!

And then I saw myself and others in heaven. We were on the sides of the aisle saying our "thank yous" and cheering Jesus while He walked down the aisle in heaven. Jesus was in His white robe, smiling at us as He walked in victory.

> Let them give glory to the Lord and proclaim his praise in the islands. The Lord will march out like a champion, like a warrior, he will stir up his zeal; with a shout he will raise the battle cry and will triumph over his enemies.
>
> —Isaiah 42:12–13 (NIV)

I can't forget what I felt when I saw Jesus walking down that aisle in victory. I was in awe to see my Hero. I was in awe to see my God.

While He was walking in the center of that aisle, I saw Him very happy to see us in heaven. I imagined Him saying, "Hey, you're worth it. And I'm so happy to see you here."

Jesus wants us in heaven, my friend. He wants you in heaven.

In the past, I thought that if I'd do more good works, then maybe I would be allowed to get to heaven. But when I saw this vision, I was reminded that indeed, you and I will not be able to get to heaven just through our own good works. God loves us so much that He poured out His own blood as a sacrifice to pay for the penalties of our sins, so that we can be with Him in heaven.

> For it is by grace you have been saved, through faith—and this is not from yourselves, it is the gift of God—not by works, so that no one can boast.
>
> —Ephesians 2:8–9 (NIV)

Jesus answered, "I am the way and the truth and the life. No one comes to the Father except through me.

—John 14:6 (NIV)

We are made right with God by placing our faith in Jesus Christ. And this is true for everyone who believes, no matter who we are. For everyone has sinned; we all fall short of God's glorious standard. Yet God, in His grace, freely makes us right in His sight. He did this through Christ Jesus when He freed us from the penalty for our sins. For God presented Jesus as the sacrifice for sin. People are made right with God when they believe that Jesus sacrificed his life, shedding his blood. This sacrifice shows that God was being fair when He held back and did not punish those who sinned in times past for He was looking ahead and including them in what He would do in this present time. God did this to demonstrate His righteousness, for He himself is fair and just, and He makes sinners right in His sight when they believe in Jesus.

—Romans 3:22–26 (NLT)

God Desires to Be with You in Heaven; Will You Say Yes to His Invitation?

God loves you so much, my friend.

You may think that God is an angry God who just wants you to do the right thing all the time, otherwise, you'll be punished for disobedience. Or you may also think that He's a killjoy who is opposed to the idea of you having fun. God is far from both. He is a loving, fun-to-be-with Father who deeply cares about you and who wants you to have the best life here on earth and in heaven.

Since Adam and Eve ate the forbidden fruit in the garden, sinning became part of mankind's nature. We have all been separated from God because of our sins. Separation from God means condemnation and suffering in hell after the death of our physical bodies. Sadly, even our good works will not be able to save us from this punishment.

But because of God's so much love for us, He became man in the person of Jesus Christ to pay for everything that is required, to buy us back from this terrifying state. God became man so that as a man, He would be able to take the punishment of death on our behalf. Jesus' death destroyed that gap between God and us. And then three days after his death, He rose again, giving us victory over death. So, we can now go to heaven and be with God!

He was thinking of you personally when He made this sacrifice. You matter to Him so much and He wants you to be saved. He's already done the sacrifice needed so that you can be with Him in heaven. **You just need to accept Him as your Savior and Lord, and you will be saved.**

You don't have to be perfect. You might feel that you're not good enough or too sinful right now to come into the arms of a Holy God. But please know that nothing is too dirty for our loving Dad in heaven. (He didn't even mind becoming a human being who would go through a gruesome death on the cross, so that His blood would be able to cleanse our dirt.) Just come home. Please come home. He is desperate for you, and your return will really make Him very happy.

I hope you can pray this prayer with me:

Dear Lord,

Thank You so much for your love for me. It's overwhelming, Lord. I don't deserve it. But thank you.

Lord, I have sinned against You for so many times. I'm so sorry. I am not clean, Lord, but will you make me clean, please? Please forgive me for all my sins.

I believe Lord Jesus that you died on the cross to pay for the penalties of my sins. Thank you for rescuing me. Thank you as because of it, I can now be with You for eternity.

Lord Jesus, I surrender my life to You. You are my Savior, my Lord, and my God. Please come into my heart and lead me as I follow you all the days of my life.

Amen.

God and all His angels are now rejoicing in heaven! If you asked Him to be the Lord of your life, He would dwell in you. And the void in your heart, which you thought needed to be filled, will be filled by the One who really owns it.

I encourage you to speak to God every day through prayer, read the Bible, and attend a Bible-based church that can help you with your walk with Him.

> Because, if you confess with your mouth that Jesus is Lord and believe in your heart that God raised him from the dead, you will be saved.
>
> —Romans 10:9 (ESV)

> Repent, then, and turn to God, so that your sins may be wiped out, that times of refreshing may come from the Lord.
>
> —Acts 3:19 (NIV)

> For God so loved the world, that He gave His one and only Son, that whoever believes in Him shall not perish, but have eternal life.
>
> —John 3:16 (NIV)

Bible: The Golden Book from God

I also would like to share with you the revelation I have received about the Bible.

It was one of those nights when I was too lazy to read my Bible. I was inside my room, working on my computer. Then I noticed that my Bible, which was placed on top of my bedside table, suddenly glowed with a bright light. If you're familiar with the cartoons entitled "Superbook" from the early 1980s, there was a part there when the Superbook (or the Bible) suddenly glows and a bright white light comes out from it—what I saw was similar to that.

The cover of my Bible, which originally had a light-blue color, suddenly turned to gold. Originally smaller, it then became four times bigger in my sight. It also became hardbound, and it appeared with engravings that made it look like a book of the King. My jaw dropped when I saw it.

I watched this scene for almost ten minutes. After seeing this supernatural scene, I realized that the Bible is indeed, *God's Holy Book*. It is not just a collection of manuscripts that were written by men. It is a sacred book that contains God's words for us.

Please read your Bible. Please read it with reverence. It's God's love letter for us.

All Scripture is God-breathed and is useful for teaching, rebuking, correcting and training in righteousness, so that the servant of God may be thoroughly equipped for every good work.

—2 Timothy 3:16–17 (NIV)

He replied, "Blessed rather are those who hear the word of God and obey it."

—Luke 11:28 (NIV)

For the word of God is alive and powerful. It is sharper than the sharpest two-edged sword, cutting between soul and spirit, between joint and marrow. It exposes our innermost thoughts and desires.

—Hebrews 4:12 (NLT)

Be Baptized

I also encourage you to be baptized. I want to share with you my baptism story.

I was inside my room one night when I heard God speak to me again. *"Be baptized."* I was surprised when I heard this message from the Lord. I've seen adult people get baptized, but I no longer thought of doing it myself, as I was already baptized as a child. To be honest, it was not easy for me to obey the Lord straight away on this instruction. I knew I wanted to surrender myself to Him, but I thought then that adult baptism meant joining a specific religion.

But the Lord was persistent. So, I checked again what's written in the Bible about baptism, and here's what I have gathered:

> Jesus came and told his disciples, "I have been given all authority in heaven and on earth. Therefore, go and make disciples of all the nations, <u>baptizing them in the name of the Father and the Son and the Holy Spirit</u>. Teach these new disciples to obey all the commands I have given you. And be sure of this: I am with you always, even to the end of the age."
>
> —Matthew 28:18–20 (NLT)

> Whoever believes and is baptized will be saved, but whoever does not believe will be condemned.
>
> —Mark 16:16 (NIV)

> Going under the water was a burial of your old life; coming up out of it was a resurrection, God raising you from the dead as he did Christ. When you were stuck in your old sin-dead life, you were incapable of responding to God. God brought you alive—right along with Christ! Think of it! All sins forgiven, the slate wiped clean, that old arrest warrant canceled and nailed to Christ's cross.
>
> —Colossians 2:12–14 (MSG)

> I baptize you with water for repentance. But after me comes one who is more powerful than I, whose sandals I am not worthy to carry. He will baptize you with the Holy Spirit and fire.
>
> —Matthew 3:11 (NIV)

I learned then that water baptism is a public declaration of our faith in and commitment to our Lord Jesus Christ. It is similar to a wedding day, which is the public display of one's commitment of marriage to his spouse. This is different however from the actual commitment of marriage. We don't get saved through baptism, but it is an outward display of our commitment to Jesus.

In baptism, being dipped into the water symbolizes the burial of our old sinful self and coming out of the water symbolizes our new life with Jesus.

I said yes to the Lord and got baptized on February 8, 2015.

When I came out of the water, I felt like I got married—to the One who has loved me without measure, and to Him who has promised "I Am with you always" and has faithfully kept it.

Epilogue

The stories which I have shared with you in the previous pages are true. I testify that they really happened.

Before receiving these revelations, I have always believed that there is a God who loves us. But I never imagined that He is just very near and that He loves us far more than anyone can ever love us.

The Bible says that no sin will be able to enter heaven. Since all of us have sinned, by default, none of us will be able to enter heaven. Through a supernatural experience, I learned that there is a state of being separated from God (or spiritual death) which all of us are subject to, as a result of our sins—the Bible also confirms this. The Bible also mentions that because of our sins, we're also subject to eternal torment in hell.

God loves us so much that He would do anything to save us from this death and eternal torment. That's why God became man two thousand years ago through Jesus Christ to pay for the penalties of our sins by dying a horrible death on the cross. His blood which was offered in that cross became our ticket so that we will be able to go to heaven, be spared from the penalties of our sins and be with God for eternity.

All we need to do is to just accept Jesus Christ as our Savior and Lord, and we will be saved.

'Accepting Jesus's Lordship' means entrusting our lives to Him and accepting Him as God who has authority over us. It means following His will; and being sorry for our sins and turning away from them. It doesn't mean that we're expected to be perfect—we will never be perfect while we're still here on earth. But accepting Jesus' Lordship means having the desire in your heart to follow

Him, acting on it and deciding to leave anything which is not pleasing to Him. Turning away from sin is definitely not an easy task, and God understands that. That's why we need God's Holy Spirit to enable us to change. Just humble yourself and ask God to help you break free from sin, and He will help you with your struggles. You'll notice how He will transform you little by little until you reach the best version of you—the person whom He has planned you to be.

Also, as God has forgiven us from our sins, He wants us to forgive. Again, it's hard, but we can ask Him to help us out if we're struggling in this area.

I also learned that there is an enemy (or the devil) who hates God and us, and who wants us to remain separated from God, and to eventually go to hell. He's very active right now in deceiving us and convincing us that God doesn't love us and that what he offers is better than what God wants for our lives. It's a lie. What he's offering is a bait which will lead to our destruction. Resist his offer—he wants you to be destroyed. God, on the other hand, wants you to have the best life here on earth and in heaven. Don't ever be afraid of the devil—God is far above him, and he's doomed to be punished in hell.

God has always loved us. He rescued us from hell even though it required Him to take our place in this punishment. Know that He never stopped loving us after He gave Himself up for us in that cross. Up to now, He lovingly stares at us for 24 hours a day, sings love songs to us, listens to us, provides for our needs and does everything which hopefully will make us realize that He cares for us. He has never left us even in our brokenness, and He has great plans for our future.

God wants to have a relationship with you, and for you to be with Him for eternity. Please say yes to Him.

He'll be delighted if you'll speak to Him in prayer, and if you'll get to know Him more by reading His Word (called the Bible).

Know that even before you knew Him, He has always loved you. And as He has promised, He is with you always.

About the Author

Perla Apolonio was born and raised in Manila, Philippines, and now lives in Sydney, Australia. She has worked as an accountant and as an IT professional for the past twenty years.

Perla grew up believing in and loving God. She was fourteen years old when she witnessed how her dad miraculously woke up from a comatose state, just after he was prayed for by her mom. Even though her dad woke up from coma that day, there were still countless times when he was rushed to the hospital in the years thereafter. These years were not easy for their family, but it was through this season that allowed Perla to know God as a powerful and living God who never leaves us or abandons us.

She has always believed that regardless of the ups and downs in life, there's an amazing God, whom we may not see, but has been faithfully looking after us. She never expected that one fateful day of June 8, 2014, she would be blessed to have a supernatural encounter with the Lord Jesus Christ. This experience has taught her that indeed, God is real, that He loves us very much and that He is with us always. She shares her testimony in this book.

In 2019, she took up and completed a course on Bible, Mission and Ministry in a Theological College in Sydney.

Acknowledgments

To my family and friends who have encouraged me, provided me with comments on the manuscript, and continuously prayed for me during this season of writing, thank you, and I pray that the Lord will bless you more than you can ever imagine. This includes Myra Apolonio, Victoria Lee, Lynn Ang, Aimee Uy, Elayne Lim, Yenn Xin, Renee Sun, Priscillia Tolentino, Pastors Ariel and Jesalyn Bernardo, Sharmine and Ian Butac, Pastor Rollie Otome, Jazel Tanghian, Angela Lau, Lester and Avril Calingasan, Jane Pontillas, Evelyn Talamayan, Jan Ceballos and many more whose names I may not be able to explicitly mention here. It was a great privilege to serve the Lord alongside with you guys in this endeavor.

To the following musical geniuses who have originally written the songs which I have included in this book, I give you so much gratitude sir/s:

- Tony Harrell and Randy Van Warmer, the writers of the song "Write Your Name (Across My Heart)," which was performed by Kenny Rogers
- Jim Brickman, David Grow, and Roch Voisine, the writers of the song "My Love Is Here," which was performed by Jim Brickman
- Steven Curtis Chapman, the writer and singer of the song "I Will Be Here" (Copyright © 1989 Sparrow Song (BMI) Greg Nelson Music (BMI) Universal Music - Brentwood Benson Songs (BMI) (adm. in Australia and New Zealand by SHOUT! Music Publishing) All rights reserved. Used by permission.)

- Van Morrison, the writer, and singer of the song "Have I Told You Lately"(© Copyright 1989 Barrule UK Ltd. All Rights Administered by BMG Rights Management (Australia) Pty Ltd Print rights administered in Australia and New Zealand by Hal Leonard Australia Pty Ltd ABN 13 085 333 713 Used By Permission. All Rights Reserved. Unauthorized Reproduction is Illegal)
- Billy Joel, the writer, and singer of the song "Just the Way You Are"
- James Weatherly, the writer of the song "This is a Love Song," which was performed by Bill Anderson
- Kerry Chater and George Robertson, the writers of the song "I O U," which was performed by Lee Greenwood
- Andrew Lloyd Webber, Charles Elliott Hart, and Richard Stilgoe, the writers of the song "All I Ask of You"
- Lionel Richie, the writer and singer of the song "Truly"
- Rey Valera, the writer, and singer of the song "*Walang Kapalit*"

To the lovely coordinators of WestBow press who have patiently guided me as I write this book, "*I Am with You Always*"; to Getty Images for the beautiful photo used at the front cover; and to my dear friend Elayne Lim for helping me with the cover design—thank you!

To my loving parents, Mom and Dad, especially Dad who will no longer be able to physically read this book but was used by God so that I'd be able to easily understand what a good father is like—thank you *po*. I love you both Mom and Dad.

Thank you so much all from the bottom of my heart.

And to our Daddy God who has loved us lavishly and sacrificed everything He has so that we will be able to see Him face-to-face in heaven one day—there are not enough words to thank You, our dear Father! Your name be glorified forever, Lord. Amen.

Printed in the United States
By Bookmasters